POETRY now

EVERCHANGING SEASONS

Edited by

Joanne Baxter

First published in Great Britain in 2000 by
POETRY NOW
Remus House,
Coltsfoot Drive,
Woodston,
Peterborough, PE2 9JX
Telephone (01733) 898101
Fax (01733) 313524

All Rights Reserved

Copyright Contributors 1999

HB ISBN 0 75430 825 1
SB ISBN 0 75430 826 X

FOREWORD

Although we are a nation of poets we are accused of not reading poetry, or buying poetry books. After many years of listening to the incessant gripes of poetry publishers, I can only assume that the books they publish, in general, are books that most people do not want to read.

Poetry should not be obscure, introverted, and as cryptic as a crossword puzzle: it is the poet's duty to reach out and embrace the world.

The world owes the poet nothing and we should not be expected to dig and delve into a rambling discourse searching for some inner meaning.

The reason we write poetry (and almost all of us do) is because we want to communicate: an ideal; an idea; or a specific feeling. Poetry is as essential in communication, as a letter; a radio; a telephone, and the main criteria for selecting the poems in this anthology is very simple: they communicate.

CONTENTS

Autumn Woods	S H Smith	1
Summer Departs	Edith Mary Lainton	2
Daisies Around A Chain	Kenny Swanston	3
Rebirth From The Remnants Of Winter	Ann G Wallace	4
Summers	Sylvia Greenland	5
Seasons	Naomi Elisa Price	6
The Week Before Christmas	Jackie M Creek	8
Winter	Coleen Bradshaw	9
Cash For A Cradle	Perry McDaid	10
Metamorphosis Of Spring	Derek Beavis	12
Autumn	Sheila Burnett	13
Seasons In A Glass	Christine Licence	14
Winter Moods	Wyn Downs	15
The Seasons	Agnes Boyd	16
No Leaves Left	Mark Young	17
Autumn	Vanessa Bell	18
Freshness Of Autumn	S Mullinger	19
The Seasons	Robert Gerald	20
The Best Time Of All	Joy Cooke	21
Winter	Jessica Utton	22
Thoughts For The Seasons	Alma Montgomery Frank	23
Autumn Chill	Ali Sebastian	24
The Garden's Song	E K Whitty	25
All Change	Denny Rhymer	26
Changing Seasons	Susan Roffey	27
Spring In Palestine	Joy Ottewill	28
Snow	Heather Currey	29
Thoughts For The Season - The Four Seasons	Donna Minto	30
September	Patricia Whiting	31
Winds Of March	Mae Cadman	32
Winter Syndrome	Elizabeth Lee	33
Winter	Mary W Roberts	34
What Comes Around	Barry Walker	35
Colours Of Autumn	P Edwards	36

Winter Suicide	Paddy Murphy	37
Golden Harvest	J E Friday	38
Seasons Of Life	Mary Skelton	39
A Season For Change	Mark Lyons	40
The Passing Of Autumn	Haidee Williams	41
The Coming Of Winter	Thelma J Lougher	42
On The Western Front	Marylène Walker	43
Summer's Passing	Sheila J Leheup	44
Winter's Spring	John Amsden	45
Summer Breeze	Alan Jones	46
I Have A Dream Of Hallowe'en In New England	Andréa Selina Bennett	47
Golden Rain	Catherine Reay	48
A Lovely Day	Ann Hathaway	49
Dance Of The Seasons	Elizabeth Amy Johns	50
Autumn	Veronica Tilbury	51
Where's It Gone?	Wendy Stark	52
Fun In The Snow	Bonita Hall	53
Autumn	Jeanette McKee	54
April's Spur	Andria J Cooke	55
High Rise	John H Hope	56
Winter	Joanne Phillips	57
Untitled	Lionel Harmsworth	59
The Country	Gwen Tipper	60
Re-birth	H Val Horsfall	61
Memories	C Cook	62
Autumn	Helen Arnold	63
Summer Storm	I McGregor	64
Fiery Autumn	David Barnett	65
Heavenly Bauble	Graham R Mann	66
My Four Seasons	Corinne Lovell	67
Autumn	Joanna John	68
Autumn Into Millennium	Kathleen Mary Scatchard	69
Winter	Pat Derbyshire	70
Summer	Joan Gray	71
Spring Senses	K P Watch	72
Autumn Dreams	Sara Harris	73
Ladies Of The Seasons	Katie Hill	74

Rain In December	Bridget Rayner	75
Comes November	Harold Hyman	76
Winter	P N Vout	77
A Place To Sit (Spring)	Paul Robards	78
Spring Again	Anne Goldson	79
Summer Rain	Roy V Whitlock	80
Walking The Four Seasons	Edgar Wall	81
His Presence	Jenny Eleftheriades	82
Beauty	Christine Ormrod	83
Year	Ian Coxall	84
Winter's Ambassador	Barry Jones	85
Autumn	Audrey Willis	86
Sounds Of Summer	Joy Adams	87
Waiting	Mary Josephine Devlin	88
Song Of The Seasons	Eileen Naish	89
Autumn Leaves	James West	90
Winter's Day	Kate Machean	91
Summer Haar	Helen Logie	92
Spring Awakening	Heida	93
It's A Mystery	J W Hewing	94
A Touch of Frost	M J Swain	95
Autumn	G W Bailey	96
Of What Was	Doris Hoole	97
November Rain	Anne Sanderson	98
Days	Valerie Ryan	99
A Change In The Weather	Helen Allison	100
A Song For Summer	Jenny Pearce	101
Images Of Autumn	John Taylor	102
Hail, Glorious Day!	Frank L Appleyard	103
Springtime In England	Mollie Fribbens	104
Autumn Garden	John F Petrie	105
The Last Rose	Denise E Wain	106
The Harvest Tree	John A Gordon	107
The Year	Graham L	108
Seasons	Doris E Farran	109
First Day Of Autumn	Frankie Bell	110
Snowing, Blowing, Raining Hard	Keith L Powell	111
The Autumn Blackberry	Joan E Blissett	112

Autumn Glory	Mary Rose Samm	113
Miracle	Tony Coyle	114
Autumn	D Linnett	115
Thanksgiving	Jim Sargant	116
Autumnal Thoughts	Terry Burrows	117
The Laughables	Louise O'Keeffe	118
Remember Winter	Patricia Harding	119
The Best Things In Life Are Free	Brenda Irene Piper	120

AUTUMN WOODS

Today, sweet chamber music filled
These autumn woods with fresh desire,
As blazing, russet raptures killed
My consciousness with tongues of fire;
And summer's leavings seemed to chart
The secret breathings of my heart.

This sighing cadence brought to me
Long rhapsodies of halcyon days -
A jewel from the planished sea
Of memory, where such beauty strays;
The oracle of tree and leaf
Intoned a requiem for my grief.

For in each leaf I saw the face
Of golden girls I knew too well,
Enshrined in this dark, Celtic place,
And still I felt the ocean swell
Of sorrows down the flood of years
That brought my universe to tears.

And, one by one, each pallid shade
Assailed my silent Pentecost;
Re-visioned through the haunted glade,
The ripened ventures of the lost
In sad procession passed me by
In dreams where crimson glories lie.

And so the autumn legend grows:
Next year the ancient tale will chime,
And crown, before the winter snows,
The diadem of wasted time;
The folklore of the soul spent year
Is ashes, yet forever here.

S H Smith

SUMMER DEPARTS

Summer sighs and sheds her garments
Faded finery scattered low
Through misty days we see the splendour
Of the autumn pageant now.
Cherry trees whose bridal blossom
Cloaked the branches in the spring
Then they bore a luscious burden
Now cloth of gold as did a king.
Green hedgerows change their coat to crimson.
Midst thorny couch the blackberries lie.
Spikes of orange, red and ochre
Pierce the gloom and light the sky.
Soon frosty hands will wipe the palette
And trees forlorn and naked stand.

Edith Mary Lainton

Daisies Around a Chain

Each day has but one life
Born with the passing of night
Dawn being its infancy
with midmorning its divine grace
Maturing with the passing of afternoon
and the diminishing of daylight
Evening carries dusk to its midnight fate

The seasons pursue each other as though daisies around a chain
Spring brings with it the grace of promise
The promise of summer's gentle days and tranquil nights
With the blessing of sunshine and clear blue skies
People's faces are brighter, their smiles wider
Their spirits warmer with the climate
They go about their routines slower
and think less of competing.

Autumn a time to retain the majesty of late summer
and prepare for the oncoming of winter
With the delights of the festive season beckoning
While still enjoying the aftermath of summer's easy pace
Gathering momentum with the breeze
that blows the leaves from the trees
and sweeps the clouds through the sky.

Winter's authority takes over with the demise of the year
Its earthy presence felt with shorter days and longer nights
Daylight can be precious during these severe months
but can still sparkle like a mountain stream
as snowflakes cover the ground like icing sugar
upon a cake.

Kenny Swanston

REBIRTH FROM THE REMNANTS OF WINTER

Winter's sculpture stands free,
Unadorned,
Stark gnarled branches,
Reach out gasping,
At the icy breath of air,

Icing sugar frost,
Paints her brush along the fingers,
Of this skeleton hand,
Once clad,
In garment of green,

Vermilion hips upon the briar,
Tempt the robin from his lair,
While a carpet white,
Lays thick upon the ground,
Ready to melt at leisure,

Soon buds appear and fill each stem,
In anticipation,
The imminent arrival of Spring,
Shows her hand,
And warmth fills the cold earth,

She waits with her garment green,
To give birth to her seed once more,
A rebirth from the ashes,
Then the skeleton remains,
Once more take form.

Ann G Wallace

SUMMERS

Summers stretch a long way,
further than the sum of time
from one equinox to the next.
More than the waiting for the sun,
the holidays, the highlights.
Even beyond the endless rain,
and boots in sodden gardens.

One summer is all summers,
all hopes of warmth and abundance,
one becoming the other,
past and future melded.

Summer is hope for the future,
remembrance of things that have gone
and time disappearing.

Sylvia Greenland

SEASONS

Seasons change
My heart stays the same
For who and what I'm really into . . .
Like you.

People come and go
Styles stop or flow
Leaves may alter their shade
And my life may again
Be rearranged.

You'll always mean the same
And as our lives never stay the same
I'll always have the same love
For you.
Though I guarantee this will grow.

What I need for you to be.
Is strong for me.
As the summer sun
Or winter rain.
It's not just one part of you I need.
Else I might refrain.

But most of all
I need to know
My heart you'll keep.

Just as I do with yours.

I'm getting more used
To people looking at me now
The more I perform
Like thunder in a storm
Though I'm not at all that grand.

You're getting more accustomed now
To me
The more I'm open with myself
When you're around.

I'm getting more into my work again now
Like the girl He's made me to be.
Not just swimming an empty sea.
Not just another leaf hanging on a tree.

Naomi Elisa Price

THE WEEK BEFORE CHRISTMAS

A time -
Of frozen locks, non starting cars,
Traffic jams, and endless queues,
Freezing fog, black ice and snow
Journeys fraught with choking fumes.
Of shopping malls and car parks full,
Shelves stacked with gifts and sold out toys
Faulty goods and lost receipts,
Harassed faces, aching feet.
Presents to get and cards to post,
Oh, and Tracy's new baby - mustn't forget.
Prams and pushchairs, screaming kids,
Pushing, shoving, go with the flow,
Gifts to wrap, a tree to trim,
Fairy lights - must check those bulbs,
Tinsel, baubles and drawing pins,
Mistletoe and holly, wreaths for the dead.
Things to make and cakes to bake,
Plus extra food - unexpected guests,
Whisky, Port and Sherry,
Fruit juice for the kids - oh!
That reminds me - Jackie's party
Oh gosh! It's fancy dress.
Now what else have I got to get?
There's just so much to do
A - A - A - Choo - oh yes!
A bout of ill timed flu.

Jackie M Creek

WINTER

Winter comes between
Autumn and
Spring
Then can
Bring the
Snow, March winds
Along with
Lots of
April showers
Also together some
Sunshine hours
In the
Wintertime
The leaves
Are no longer
On the
Trees
In the winter
Breeze.

Coleen Bradshaw

CASH FOR A CRADLE

Christmas approaches, the shops stores swell -
with season's cockroaches racing to hell.
The Spirit of Christmas in which I once revelled
has somehow been lost; my soul's landscape levelled.

Has it been neglected, or do I err -
am I the insensate, does everyone else care?
I find myself drifting, my morals shifting;
still I cling to ideals uplifting.

Back from my reverie, I watch those pale faces
intent on their shopping in Dunne's and Mace's;
unseeing eyes checking off minds' lists -
Jesus forgotten 'midst commerce's mist!

A toy fox for Julie, 'Turtle' for John -
a catalogue of orders that goes on and on;
must not go home without the mince pies,
and some 'Baby Bio' in case that plant dies!

Home now, make sure the kids go to bed -
up early for Mass, despite Dad's sore head.
We'll go 8.00 am, get it out of the way -
there's so much on TV, I hope mother won't stay!

She's gone, can relax, bring out the wine -
it will settle our stomachs! The meal was just fine!
Collapse in a heap in front of the set -
hubby studies 'form' for tomorrow's big bet!

The TV is on and the presents uncovered -
should clean the dishes; couldn't be bothered.
'Mummy, who's Jesus?' Julie hugs her toy fox.
'Hush now, dearest, I'm watching the box!'

John walks his turtle across the carpeted floor,
says 'Jesus is a little boy - He's terribly poor!
He lives in the church and is lonely tonight,
for it is His birthday - Mommy, isn't that right?
Mommy - isn't that right?

Perry McDaid

METAMORPHOSIS OF SPRING

This brighter light which shines with greater force,
Expels from earth the frost which yet does cling,
And speeds dark winter's night upon its course,
And lifts the gloom to welcome back the spring.
The trees in bud await their smart attire,
And cajoles men to marvel at the scene.
Bedecked with form and beauties which inspire,
Those writers who from nature's works will glean.
Their spirits lifted, hearts of men give praise,
At earth transformed by glories which entice,
With sights and views to make all voices raise.
The land conforms; resembling paradise.
When winter's dead, and spring's new life abounds,
Then men can feel that earth with hope resounds.

Derek Beavis

AUTUMN

Every season has its beauty,
Has its colours, has its moods,
Wrought by God, they ring the changes,
Making everything brand new.

Days for planting, weeks for growing,
Spring and summer brightly dressed,
Sparkling whiteness in the winter;
But it's autumn I love best.

Autumn garners all the goodness
Of the months that go before,
Then it adds a hint of sadness
For the past will come no more.

Gone the brightness, gone the glory,
Autumn's tones are brown and gold,
Yet the trees with fruit are laden
To sustain us through the cold.

So in nature, as in living -
All our middle years abound
With God's blessings tinged by sadness,
Just like autumn all year round.

Sheila Burnett

SEASONS IN A GLASS

If we could catch the seasons and put them in a glass.
The colours we would capture would last, and last, and last.
Each time you looked upon the glass, your life would surely change, as
Winter time and summer time was mixed up with the rain.

The glass would make you happy sometimes make you sad, but it will
Bring back memoirs of the season that we've had.
Seasons with their many charms, cold and bright and warm.
Summer days, lazy days, the cold and frosty morn.

The leaves so golden on the trees, the snow so white and crisp.
The conkers, and the acorns, and Jack Frost's crispy mist.
The seasons are so magical they come and go so fast. We would not
Want to trap them not even in a glass.

Christine Licence

Winter Moods

How I long for the first sign that spring is on its way.
For weeks it's been winter with gloom all day.
The wind moaning in the tree tops and up in the eaves
Whistling round the corners, throwing up the leaves.
Looking out my window and peering through the rain
All seems so depressing, will the sunshine come again?
Putting on my coat and boots, I decide to face the storm.
I hoped that I would see, a sign that spring would soon be born.
Through the cold, mud and puddles, and the pouring rain.
I set off to see a cottage garden, that I knew was up the lane.
I knew that from winters past the treasures I would find.
Snowdrops and acconites, the sight would ease my mind.
I looked over the bare hedgerow, and across the lawn.
There in a sheltered corner was my hope of spring, reborn.
Like ballerinas dancing in skirts of white and green
In the wind they bowed to one another, as though acting
                                          out some scene.
With the bright yellow of the acconites, becoming the
                                          décor of the stage.
For a while, I stood there gazing as the winter tempest raged.
Then I retraced my steps homeward, feeling peace within my heart.
Knowing that these winter days, before long would depart.

Wyn Downs

THE SEASONS

The first flowers of Spring are beginning to show
Just above ground, surrounded by snow,
Soon they will burst into colourful life
Surviving again through cold winter's knife.

Then comes the Summer and the warm sun
Brightens the days, the children have fun
Down on the beaches, or out in the parks,
Carefree, laughing, playful as larks.

Next comes the Autumn when the trees seem to say,
Our leaves are all colours, and fall when we sway,
We're feeling quite tired, it's time for a rest,
The colours of Autumn are the ones I like best.

Back comes the Winter with cold winds and snow
That covers the ground where flowers used to grow,
When snowmen are built, and Christmas is near,
But Spring will return and we'll start a new year.

Agnes Boyd

No Leaves Left

Gail's fingers are pulling off leaves.
A dizzy weather-vane keeps spinning.
Gather around the greedy bonfire.

Wind's rock the masts of trees.
Through keyholes its breath is whistling.
Tongues of flame are licking higher.

Here, there's no gentle breeze.
Pegged clothes are line dancing.
Gather around the greedy bonfire.

Gusts shriek like countless banshees.
Flags and sails and tents are flapping.
Tongues of flame are licking higher.

You're tugging at jackets, trousers and sleeves.
A black bin goes rocking then rolling.
Gather around the greedy bonfire.

Skirts are lifted above blue knees.
The fists of the waves keep pounding.
Tongues of flame are licking higher.
Gather around the greedy bonfire.

Mark Young

AUTUMN

A crisp, cold autumn morning
A hazy sun shines from above
A gauzy mist hangs in the air
This is the time of year I love

Upon the bare ploughed fields
Gather woodpigeons, rooks and crows
To search for the precious food they need
To see them through the winter snows

A silent cascade of autumn leaves
Falls silently to the ground
A myriad of colour
Yellow, orange, russet, brown

The bare boughs of the naked trees
Reach upwards to the sky
And down below on a carpet of leaves
A squirrel scampers by

For he is on an urgent quest
Before the snow comes down
To find as many nuts as he can
And bury them in the ground

And as the sun begins to set
And the mist descends from above
The birds go to roost,
The trees become silhouettes,
It's the time of year I love.

Vanessa Bell

FRESHNESS OF AUTUMN

I love to feel crisp leaves beneath my feet,
Autumn, beautiful with blackberries sweet.
This is the best season, this I adore,
Differing colours and smells, who wants more.
Warm enough to drink coffee in the sun,
And go on long walks, when days work is done.
Freshness of autumn can never be beat,
Afraid other seasons cannot compete.

S Mullinger

THE SEASONS

Trees in full bud as we welcome spring,
green grasses swaying in a gentle breeze,
a blackbird perched on a tree does sing,
hedges alive with the humming of bees.
Raindrops shining like a thousand jewels,
colourful flowers with sweet scented petals.

The rumble of thunder and flashes of lightning,
heralding the coming of a summer storm,
the glorious red of a sunset sky,
as day with a fanfare to night says goodbye,
all the heavens are alight with a shroud of stars,
the serenity of a silver moon kissing the water.

A lowering sun on a crisp autumn day,
soon it will be too cold for the children to play,
deep grey mists veiling the midday sun,
the gliding of herons in slow motion,
lowering of cattle in the distant meadow,
a flight of wild geese as homeward they go.

Winter approaches bringing pearls of snow,
as I sit alone by a firelight glow,
windows gleaming with bone white frost,
and crystal icicles do carpet the grass,
thunderous clouds roaming across the black sky,
stinging rain on your face like an icy spray.

How quickly the seasons seem to pass by.

Spring came along and had its say,
Summer followed in the same old way,
Autumn so colourful did it's best,
To prepare us for winter and it's discontent.

Robert Gerald

The Best Time Of All

How we love the lights at Christmas
Shining on the tree.
Singing Christmas carols
With friends and family.
The joyful shouts of children.
The presents and hot mince pies.
The sights and smells of Christmas.
The warm glow in everyone's eyes.
We think of the star of Bethlehem,
And the stable where Jesus was born
And placed within a manger,
That cold, cold winter's morn.
We think of those now gone from us,
And those so far away.
In our hearts we are together,
Because it's Christmas Day.

Joy Cooke

WINTER

Summer is ending,
Winter is coming.
Light disappears.
It becomes dark.
Sitting at home
In the living room,
Coldness comes.
Snuggling up in bed
Hearing the rain fall.
It is the end of summer
And winter begins.

Jessica Utton (11)

THOUGHTS FOR THE SEASONS

Every season has something to be joyful over
Spring with its beautiful delicate flowers
Summer with its day of perpetual sunshine
Autumn with its crimson, red and green trees
Winter with its snow, ice, frost and bitter winds
But the best day of all is Christmas Day
When Jesus Christ was born to Mary
A millennium ago!

Alma Montgomery Frank

AUTUMN CHILL

The dreaded cold is back again
things are just not the same.
For a country with both,
freezing winters and steamy summers
people never get used to these dilemmas.

'It's a hell of a weather.'
says our vicar.

'From one extreme to another'
says our mother.

'Devil make up your mind'
says our father.

'But is it the devil or God?'
says our sister.

'It is hard to tell'
says our brother Melv.

'I think it is the devil's will,
because it was like being in an evil cell yesterday,
the way the lightning and rain fell.'
says myself.

Has Pandora's box opened a second time?
If so it is a real crime,
yet worst of all, it is a terrible sign.
I wish this madness would end today,
for winter is on its way.

Ali Sebastian

THE GARDEN'S SONG

Icy snowdrops palest hue
Dainty primrose, violet blue.
Daffodils sing loud and clear -
'All rejoice, for Spring is here.'

Crimson roses, fragrant, bloom.
Pinks distil a sweet perfume.
Hollyhocks sing loud and clear -
'All rejoice, for Summer's here.'

Rosy fruits hang on the bough,
Harvest time is with us now.
Orange leaves sing loud and clear -
'All rejoice for Autumn's here.'

Seedlings in the greenhouse warm,
Sheltering the snow and storm,
Shyly sing 'Though Winter's here
All rejoice, for Spring is near.'

E K Whitty

All Change

Autumn glory
reveals the story
of an annual event!
Scenes re-arranging,
Colours changing,
And leaves are meant
To promptly float,
and powerfully gloat:
A carpet of every hue.
Meanwhile, this season
Helps us to reason:
Nature will renew!

Denny Rhymer

CHANGING SEASONS

Fairies of the dandelion flowers
Floating by each telling hours
Teaching us summer is all but done
Ahead of us is autumnal fun

Crispy leaves beneath our feet
Halloween, for trick or treat
Into cobwebs we blindly walk
Creepy crawleys, don't give a thought

Although the sky is of palest pinks
Soon rain clouds come, so nature drinks
Flowering blooms hang their pretty heads
Once radiant in their summer beds

Festivals of harvest are thanked by all
Gathered in before the fall
Dreams of summer are passed with ease
Slipping into thoughts of Christmas . . . Festivities

Birds are returning from their rest of the season
As day to night turns from warm to freezing
No more childish laughter at play
But foggy mornings, and musty days

Soon autumn will pass; winter will come
Spring will herald summer's fun.

Susan Roffey

SPRING IN PALESTINE

The orange trees bow down
On the terraces,
And the olives
Grey green
Cluster among blood-red anemones;
There a shepherd boy
Pipes and pipes
In the clear, cold air,
And aimless sheep
Shuffle and shove their way
From rock to patchy grass,
While goats skip
Drunk in the morning sun.

Up there, in remoter air,
Monasteries hang
Their complicated life
On slabs of rock,
Weaving patterns of love,
Cultivating trees
In orderly rows;
The monks toil
And mutter orisons,
While around them Spring
Shrieks and presses
With slant of eye,
And twitch of veil.

Joy Ottewill

SNOW

Snow came down last Christmas
Soft and white and cold
Made the young feel younger
And the old feel old.

Trees seemed white with blossom
Berries hard to hold
Water's frozen over
Hungry birds grew bold.

Icicles from fountains
Lovely to behold
Glittering like diamonds
Shone in suns full gold.

Later in the moonlight
As the clouds unrolled
White had turned to silver
Silver world's unfold.

Heather Currey

THOUGHTS FOR THE SEASON - THE FOUR SEASONS

I couldn't pick a favourite, although I did try,
It's just I like all the seasons, and this is why.

A new year has come again,
Bringing the sun and leaving the rain.
Leaves are budding on the trees,
Flowers dancing in the breeze.
Birds are singing, bees are humming,
Everyone's happy because spring is coming.

Holiday time for one and all,
No more school until the fall.
The summer sun is beating down,
Turning sunbathers a golden brown.
Days at the beach, swimming in the sea,
These are the days for people like me.

Colours changing just like the season,
Autumn's arrived, that is the reason.
Red, orange, bronze and brown,
All the leaves are tumbling down.
Halloween and firework displays,
As autumn brings much shorter days.

Woolly coats now winter's here,
Christmas greetings full of good cheer.
Snowballs flying to and fro,
Children's faces all aglow,
Early to bed and early to rise,
All in aid of Santa's surprise.

Summer, winter, spring or fall,
I cannot choose, I like them all.

Donna Minto

SEPTEMBER

Golden September, the best month of the year
It's a time for thanksgiving and bringing good cheer -
The colours of autumn a joy to behold
From the rosy red apple, to leaves russet and gold.

The shiny blackberries growing on bramble
Ripe for the picking by folk who will ramble
Up hill and down dale, armed with basket and cane
Gathers them quickly in case of some rain.

The dew on the grass at first morning light
Gossamer webs glistening so bright
The stillness of morning, no sound to be heard
Until the dawn chorus and the song of the bird.

Bright orange lanterns lean to the grass,
Hydrangea blossoms, a glorious mass,
The sun it sets slowly, goes down in the west
Yes! This is the month that I love the best.

Patricia Whiting

WINDS OF MARCH

Gently blows the soft warm summer breeze - moves
Shimmering flowers - in shy tranquillity.

September's falling leaves - dance in autumn's bright
And blustery winds -

Now twist and turn with gay abandon - floating - now
Dancing with great agility

The winds of winter blow ice-cold - the season's change -
Bring rain and snow

Glowing fires warm rooms, with doors now closed to
Winter winds hostilities

Now roaring winds of march - heads promise soon
To spring's awakening

Lessened now to calm - reveals God's glory in
Nature's true abilities

Wild March winds abate, herald now the Easter message
With man's faith renewed

We accept his hand in nature's wonders
Through his humility

The March winds pass again to soft warm summer
Breeze
With faith renewed - pray that 'calm' can overcome this
Troubled world anxiety.

Mae Cadman

WINTER SYNDROME

Why do I feel so tired and low,
As a child I loved the snow,
With the sight of wind and rain,
Back to bed I go again . . .
I yawn and close my eyes for hours,
Longing for the sun and flowers,
Forget the housework . . . read a book,
Must find some energy to cook,
March is here - things look brighter,
Now the day's a little lighter,
Don't think I'm lazy - or a moan,
This dreaded thing - winter syndrome.

Elizabeth Lee

WINTER

Will she come dancing, leaping and prancing,
Raucously singing and shouting with glee;
Pounding the trees to a shuddering bending,
Whirling their leaves in a wild jamboree;
Whipping the clouds till they roar in their anguish,
And weep with the pain of her bright, searing glance;
Snatching our hats and pirouetting umbrellas,
Compelling us all to join in her dance.
Or will she come softly, not fully awakened,
Gentled by dreams still clouding her eyes,
Trailing her coverlet, patterned with snowflakes,
Over the land as the last rosebud dies.
She is beautiful then, bedecked in her ermine,
With crystals adorning her long, streaming hair,
But deep in her bosom no warm heart is beating,
For winter knows not how to love or to care.

Mary W Roberts

WHAT COMES AROUND

The joy of summer, the nights of clear
When the next day of heat seems so very near
The smell of the grass, the sky yet so blue
When the song of the birds sing forever true.

Slowly the breeze seems stronger and cold
And the days of the singing seem memories of old
Trees lose their colour the scene becomes brown
And the leaves that once were, cover the town.

More fierce the wind, the nights give nothing away
The snow on the ground rules the night and the day
No food for the wildlife, the task becomes tough
Yet the children and the snow cannot get enough.

Life starts again, survival of the few
Food is a plenty and the flowers bloom new
Nature has done the route through pleasure and pain
And the cycle of life starts all over again.

Barry Walker

COLOURS OF AUTUMN

Winds blow
Leaves rain down
Gold and brown

Bonfires burn
Fireworks explode into the sky
Gales bring piles of leaves
Blowing by

Nights get darker
The cold comes back
Placed in cider casks

Harvests gathered
Winter only weeks away
The autumn colours have their day.

P Edwards

WINTER SUICIDE

Adhesive squirrels on the nuts
Of winter beaten branches
And rain sloshed barks
Teetering on the shores
Of timeless sluggishness.

I pause at this bridge
With deafening polluting traffic
Behind me
And jump
Into freezing freedom
To eternity
Beyond the arms of brave police
Their reward humane, mine music.

Paddy Murphy

GOLDEN HARVEST

Bright and sunny is the day
There are happenings down my way
It's harvest time gather all
Wheat and barley growing tall
Glistening gold stood waist high
Are the oats and the rye
Corn buntings whistle as they fly
Skylarks high in the sky
Out with combine sickle and scythe
Reap the corn whilst its dry
Horse and cart, tractor trailer
Followed by the thumping baler
Farmer's in the golden fields
Gathering in the harvest yield

Backwards forwards to the yard
Many men working hard
Stacking sheaf's into stacks
Carrying corn in heavy sacks
Some delivered to the windmill
High upon the village hill
Millers mill the corn into flour
Working hard every hour
Bakers kneading flour to make bread
To ensure we are well fed
Corn flower blue poppy red
Wonderful sights that fill my head
I love to see the fields of gold
Just as it was in days of old.

J E Friday

SEASONS OF LIFE

Life is like the weather
With intermittent rain,
Hearts cry out in sorrow
To relieve the hidden pain -
Laughter is the sunshine
And with the early morning dew,
Refreshes, cleans . . . restores and heals
To give a clearer view.

We're patterned in with nature
And like the flowers that grow,
There comes a seasonal cleansing
With a little winter's snow -
To bloom again in springtime
When understanding grows,
Is nature's gift . . . renewal
In the springtime of our lives!

Mary Skelton

A Season For Change

My favourite time has to be April in spring
When nature's doors open, wondrous sights lie within
The beauty of flowers and the grandeur of trees
Of birds building nests and of buzzing busy bees
To walk through the dew in a morning of magic
To search on this earth for sights as majestic
The clouds in the sky are like feathers and down
As birds sing and fly high within the sun's glorious crown
The showers that fall and wash drab winter away
The fauna and flora and all is life's time to make hay
Lord leave us this moment to savour much longer
The warmth on our faces and our love that's much stronger
This time of such growth is a lesson to never forsake
Were different beliefs are our friends, has we share in life's work
As it comes to its end the good work it has done
This time when life flourishes and the peace it has won.

Mark Lyons

THE PASSING OF AUTUMN

Under a colder, clearer, sky
The leaves of autumn change and dry,
Orange and yellow, green and gold,
Clinging tightly they face the cold.
Shivering, rattling, in the trees
Defying Autumn's chilly breeze.
Red berries falling to the grass
Are eaten by the birds that pass.
Red squirrels hunt the woodland floor
For fat brown nuts to eat or store.
The winds get colder by the day.
Brown shrivelled leaves just blow away,
Swirling into the moving air,
Off blackened twigs all stripped and bare.
Cold winter like a thief has come
To steal the last of Autumn's sun.
Veils of mist from leaden skies
Are nature's tears as Autumn dies.

Haidee Williams

THE COMING OF WINTER

When the berries of the hawthorn
Hang in clusters on the bough
The frost has touched the foliage
Just gently on the brow
The gardens lost its glory
The sunshine lost its glow
And all the winter sportsmen
Are rearing for to go.

The time when all the country folk
Are destined for a change
Fishing makes a graceful bow
And shooting leaves the range
The steeple chasing starts afresh
The flat is in decline
And evenings call for glowing hearths
A book and mulling wine.

Thelma J Lougher

ON THE WESTERN FRONT

The night digs a hole
In the twilight sky,

The sun lingers bleeding
Wounded on the western front.
No one cares to pick it up

But the moon fills the space
And holds the darkness in its place

Haughty stars look down
On a patch of summer
And the cold blanket of winter.

The wind follows everything
Underage emperor on the wing.

Marylène Walker

SUMMER'S PASSING

Stay a little longer summer
Please don't fade away too soon
Lovely days spent in the garden
Picnics in the afternoon

Village fetes and country markets
Produce piled on wooden stalls
Boot sales spread across the meadow
Flower shows in tiny halls.

Goldfish glinting in the water
Of the ornamental pool
Tabby cat lies soporific
Beneath a bush to keep her cool.

Children's laughter from the garden
Playing near the sprinkler hose
Refreshing scents of mint and basil
Perfume from a crimson rose.

Autumn's waiting to take over
Cornflake-crisp the leaves descend
Chilly nights and misty mornings
Halcyon days are at an end.

Sheila J Leheup

WINTER'S SPRING

How dark the night in glittering
Silence now, the snow hushed
And still besparkled with the
Many coloured lights that glint flittering
In the shaded times sombrous
In the lost landscapes.
Yet the dawn in pale light
Seasons the black and white lustrous

In a winter's sun
Still not revealing what is lost
Nor yet what can be found
Until those steel rays shun
The secret of a planet still won
In life known or life hidden.
Not so quiet the strong winds rampage
Rage upon the tearing seas, 'ere we begun.

To view an image new
Uproot the great beauty of the trees
No spring harbour when the shining
Snows into great flows grew
But how very quiet this night
Still speaks of winter's magic
A lantern for the life and light of spring
In bird's swift flight and animal's delight.

Now no respite from nature's zeal
Where scarred and damaged it will reveal
The wintertimes will no sweet spring augur
And fear must mount in worlds made unreal.

John Amsden

SUMMER BREEZE

Her presence felt dearly
When entwined in solo dreams
Feminine touch reflects like calming sea
To seal love then heal
Sensitivity on even keel
As animals too draw closely
Togetherness like petals around scarlet rose
Nature keeps open door
Riding favoured horse
Amid greenlit meadow
At ease, summer breeze
Helps stabilise inner peace.

Alan Jones

I HAVE A DREAM OF HALLOWE'EN IN NEW ENGLAND

Witches flying through the leaves
of gold and crimson maple trees
Black cats - pointy hats
I love all that!
In New England.

Pumpkins glower in the dark
Demons wander through the park
'Trick or treat?'
On every street
In New England.

And in their ancient clapboard homes
The ghosts of whalers brood alone
Dreaming of when
There could be found
Whales across Nantucket Sound.

And while the thirsty vampires prowl
And the soulless werewolves howl
My spells I still must weave
My fate to never lead
New England.

Andréa Selina Bennett

GOLDEN RAIN

The day was slow to begin;
Half spent before the sun appeared,
But now the sky is blue,
Deep blue,
Clearer than summer's blue
And the air is crisp and clean,
Although the wind is keen
And the dew will never dry before the night;
Dripping from crimson hip and haw;
Diamonds in the grass.

Poplars sigh in the wind;
Back and forth,
Back and forth
Towering besoms sweep the sky,
While the last of their leaves
Flutter and fly,
Flutter and fly like startled birds

And all the while, the golden rain;
Leaves drifting down,
Then gathered up,
Hurled high again,
Spinning faster and faster in their final dance
And falling, leaf on leaf,
Leaf on leaf;
Green to rust and ochre faded,
But the rain is gold.

Catherine Reay

A Lovely Day

The day was warm and sunny clouds of cotton wool white
Sailed across a blue sky hills stretched way out of sight
All around us sweet countryside smells peppered the air
Corn fields danced the breezes as they welcomed us there
Herds of horned cattle shaded beneath sculptured shape't trees
Curly sheep graze the grasses and honey was made by the bees
Little white cottages miraged the horizon on this perfect day
We'd found a wonderful spot to linger the afternoon away
Kaleidoscope rays pierced through canopy giving inches of light
Woodland in summer, it's just a wonderful breath taking sight
Such a prefect place we've found quiet forests country dell
From our picnic basket wafts such a mouth watering smell
Wrapped carefully in linen squares so spotlessly white
Home made scones with jam and cream baked fluffy and light
Hard boiled eggs, bottles of home made cider labelled July 1944
We recite poetry, tell stories, play games, others go off to explore
Birds sing sweetly small animals scurry forest floor and scuffle
Busy ants with twigs and leaves too big to carry they tussle
Tiny insects dart here and there, forest bees caress my face
Swaying treetops paint pictures across sky line with such grace
Riding along country lanes homeward shadowed by coming night
Soft white clouds pass over setting sun now shading our light
Horses nibble purple hedges of roadside heather's so lazily
Reaching outskirts of the city its lights come through hazily
Our wonderful day now over etched memories now left to remind
Ride towards the city lights leaving the countryside behind.

Ann Hathaway

DANCE OF THE SEASONS

Winter brings wild storms and snow . . .
Calm days of beauty - in ebb and flow;
Log fires burning, lamps alight,
Curtains drawn, against the night.

Spring reveals a gladsome scene . . .
Fragrant blossoms . . . soft shades of green;
Life giving warmth, soft airs drifting by,
Swallows dipping and soaring
Through a clear April sky.

Summertime brings sultry days . . .
Scent of hay and ripening corn;
Hot sun filtering through the trees . . .
Heat haze rising in a rose coloured dawn.

Ripe autumn arrives in a russet gown . . .
Red gold leaves - in spiralling flight;
Sun-flushed apples still crowding the bough,
Frosty meadows shimmering
In the moon's silver light.

Each season has its beauty . . .
With bounteous gifts to bring,
But the loveliest one of all, by far . . .
Is the newly awakening spring.

Elizabeth Amy Johns

Autumn

I knew it would happen, didn't realise it so near,
Woke up this morning to find autumn's here.
Out in the countryside, over the past weeks,
Migrating birds in hundreds, hotter climate seek.
Farmers plough fields till the end of the day,
Stock barns for the winter, with straw and of hay.
Sleepy owls peer down, from rafters high above,
Chicken settle in hay bales, alongside mice and dove.
Early mornings on hedgerows, jewelled spiders webs are seen,
Bright shining red rose hips, where once dog roses had been.
Blackberries adorn prickly hedges, of newly ploughed up fields,
Excited, dashing squirrels, relieve hazels of their yields.
Through the woodland passage, a favourite of mine to go,
I smell the scent of autumn, I see the occasional doe.
Falling leaves make soft carpets, of yellow, gold and brown,
Beech nuts, conkers and chestnuts, which early frosts brought down.
Fungi and various toadstools, of many fairy tales are told,
Where goblins, fairies and pixies, lived in days of old.
For hibernating creatures, an industrious time of year,
Making safe warm havens, whilst waiting for spring to appear.
Autumn brings a calmness, a mellow and thankful heart,
The beauties of this season, I never want to part.

Veronica Tilbury

WHERE'S IT GONE?

What has happened to summer, it's gone and the wind is high.
The rain lashes down on the window and the winter's cold is nigh.
It hardly seemed to last at all this year, we always say.
But come next spring we'll forget, as the sun shines out each day.
Why do we only remember the days that are sunny and warm?
Is it because we need good times to keep us from being forlorn?
Well here's to next spring and summer I say as the light goes on.
And I pull the curtains to blot out the cold and the rain and - no sun.

Wendy Stark

FUN IN THE SNOW

When summer's doors are shut
When autumn's winds are done
Then in rolls winter with her snow
And now begins the fun

Snowmen standing proud
Gardens dressed in white
Days that all seem shorter
Than the never ending night

Hats and scarves and woolly gloves
Snowballs and sledding too
Winter is my favourite time
So many things to do

Kids sliding in the playground
Snow heavy on the trees
Cold and crispy mornings
With sun there just to tease

Snowmen melt then freeze again
Squirrels come to play
Fooled into thinking it's summer
By just one sunny day

Snowdrops poke their tiny heads
Above earth's frozen floor
They enjoy the feel of sunshine
I like the snowflakes more

I say goodbye to winter
With spring approaching fast
And it's nice to see the sunshine
But I wish the snow could last

Bonita Hall

AUTUMN

Misty gold the morning
Starts a bright October day
Gossamer cobwebs cling to trees
Where young grey squirrels play
Across the fields the secretive fox
Resplendent in his coat of red
Turns at the sound of my footstep
Then steals back to his bed
The sun peeps over the horizon
And lights the clear blue sky
In its rays I stand to watch
Rabbits scurrying by
Trees turning red and gold
Their leaves fall to the ground
Dry and light as feathers
They touch with hardly a sound
I walk through woodland paths
With crisp leaves on the ground
How wonderful to be here
When there's no one else around

Jeanette McKee

APRIL'S SPUR

Even the ancient oak puts out new leaves
Of tender green when it at last concedes
The wheel full-turned, that it must bear
Another season, another year.

The piteous bleat of distant lambs newborn
Drifts far across still, pearly fields at dawn
And countless, tiny, earthbound things
Unfold, then cuckoo-calling rings.

Huge, regal chestnuts blossom into bowers
Of billowing foliage, pale, mysterious flowers
And every soul with heart to sing
Is quickened by the whip of spring.

Andria J Cooke

HIGH RISE

These building plots are repossessed; skeletal
frameworks on an old estate,
bare scaffolding for new construction blocks;

the builders well-known firm of thickening light
and making wing to rookie woods
to cancel bonds that keep the daylight pale,

with unpaid labour on these high-rise flats
from dawn to sunset in the stretching days,
social correctness in survival partnership:

males timber-shaping, gleaning stalk and husk
for airlift cargoes, city's siege relief
brought in ceaseless sky-fleet tides,

their mates, generic crofters, weaving snug
materials into basket tangle-crèche
firm against the equinoctial gales.

Don't quail at death, just glory in the crow,
admire the black-spread pinions, wheeling glide
to village groupings, nucleated heritage.

day-bright witch claws sharp in carrion swoop
scouring the tarmac clean of offal shreds,
God's hygiene squad fresh cleansing hills and towns.

Hints of greening coarsen lines of black
as birds turn backs on final March-raw rains.
The village clusters, stilted hatching-rooms

will shade and incubate the spring day long
in scaly camouflage of webbing weave,
mocking in a nasal oboe quark and
spattering car roofs, let you know they're there.

John H Hope

WINTER

The clouds are heavy and filled with rain
Dreary November is here again
The garden's dull and damp and bare
With not a touch of colour there.
The birds are silent in the trees
Oh how I hate days such as these
And then into December the year does go
Will Christmas be frosty and white with snow
Like a Christmas card's view of long ago?
It's January and again the sky is dark
But buds are peeping in the park.
Bravely through the soil they strain
Midst January's cold and February's rain.
Little snowdrops so white and frail
Face fierce March winds and freezing hail
Then April's here with her gentle showers
Watering all the delicate flowers.
The sun breaks through and the birds now sing
A cheerful chorus to welcome the spring.

Joanne Phillips

UNTITLED

I have seen ten thousand sunsets
clouds through bare branches
and late snows lying

I curl my collar at the wind
and lean into my stride
in the cold blue dusk seagulls flying

The mackerel sky is pink now
and shadows fall long
across the snow

I glance up and the sky is darker
all the earth is losing colour
Silhouettes are most manifest and show

and speak more as symbols
due to light and dark dividing
appearing as effigies and demons

But still the sky is blue
though the sun has gone
and changeling clouds like chameleons

gather golden and red hues
Some are grey now
as if their life was gone

with the sun
Darkling becomes the sky
With clear cool blue depths beyond

now the dark has come
and so the colours go
retreating from night's birth

but day will dawn again
why should we weep
darkness fills the earth

Lionel Harmsworth

The Country

Give me the country, the woods and the meadows,
The birds and the flowers and the clear flowing stream.
Show me the lane with the quaint old farmhouse,
Where the hens and the cows give their eggs and their cream.

Give me the hills and the green of the valleys,
Let me just walk o'er the stretch of the moor.
Let me hear once again, the strange call of the curlew,
And the cry of the gulls as they make for the shore.

Give me the country, when springtime is calling,
When blossoms are bursting and lambs are at play,
And summer when bees fill the air with their humming,
And the barns are stacked high with the corn and the hay.

Oh take me away from the dust of the city,
The rush of the traffic and trample of feet.
Just give me the quiet and peace of the country,
That's where I belong for there life is sweet.

Gwen Tipper

RE-BIRTH

Through mists of time
Thoughts meander,
Recalling days
Of long ago.
Those summer days
Warm and lazy;
Rich autumn's leaves
Of red and gold;
Cold winter's rime
And burning logs;
Then spring's re-birth
With gentleness.
Misty mornings
In country lanes;
Gossamer, bright
With diamond dew;
The fresh ploughed fields
All tones of brown,
And bursting buds
On lofty trees.
Bright coloured blooms
Erupting there,
And birds' song sweet
From bush and bough;
The rural sounds
Upon the ear,
And one's mind filled
With tranquillity.

H Val Horsfall

MEMORIES

When you are feeling lonely and think nobody cares,
Think only of the good times, the fun you once did share.
When you were young and frisky, the boys and girls you used to meet,
The games you played that were risky, but really were quite sweet.
The evenings at the pictures, never mind what film was on,
Or dancing down the Welfare while Alf blew on his trumpet
And the 'rock and roll' played on.
The lovely long, hot summer days that seemed to go on forever,
The walks and picnics down Cutside are memories we must treasure.
The changing days when autumn came, when the leaves began to fall,
The nature walks along New England Lane,
The bluebells the girls gathered were like a carpet in the woods,
While the boys, their conkers gathered.
After autumn, winter came and always brought the snow.
All around were snowdrifts, they made a lovely scene.
I hope you feel much better now after our stroll down memory lane,
Oh! just a little postscript, we mustn't forget spring,
With all the pretty flowers that only spring can bring.

C Cook

Autumn

Russet and gold leaves of autumn's gown
With gusty winds come tumbling down
Laying a carpet at nature's leisure
With sounds and scents for us to treasure

There's the harvest mouse and festival of thanks
Bonfire night and childish pranks
There's Hallowe'en parties and fancy dress
Brisk walks in the park now the temperature's less

Autumn gets ready with the cooling sun
For the planters moon before winter's begun
Nature prepares for her deepest sleep
With berries for food, thick wool on the sheep

The days get shorter, skies turn grey
Rain and fog hang around all the day
Sometimes there's a sunset to make us stare
And the trees stand so proud but ever so bare

And so autumn changes her colourful display
A herald that winter is soon on its way
Always a pleasure this time of the year
As one season fades and another draws near

Helen Arnold

SUMMER STORM

The unasked for spade of smell, digs out long covered pain,
The scent of wet blue lupins, in heavy summer rain,
Brought a picture of dead ducklings, beside a path of slate,
A storm had snuffed their life out, by mere quirk of fate.

Plastered yellow feathers and curled up scaled feet,
Their tiny battered bodies, a shattered childhood treat,
The sparkle gone from now dull eyes, I wonder where it went,
It was a new experience, to see a life force spent.

To a happy four year old, each bird had been a friend,
And I could see no reason, for their untimely end,
But there amongst the flowers, in the quickly drying sun,
A child had learnt the lesson, that life was not all fun.

I McGregor

FIERY AUTUMN

The last flickers of summer still burn,
The last memories of heady days still turn.

The fire of autumn explodes with colour,
The reds and golds burn brown together.

Goodbye to long evenings and early days,
Goodbye kiss to summer's lazy haze.

Oh what passions in smells of September song,
The sweet magic of blackberries on the tongue.

It's a daunting time for winter nods,
A time to indulge warm vanilla pods.

Although autumn's come with its cold lit night,
A hug from you keeps my fire bright.

David Barnett

HEAVENLY BAUBLE

A little droplet of thaw, teetering
At the point of a green needle
While invisible beams of fire, multiply
Lending colours to a colourless ball.

Graham R Mann

My Four Seasons

Spring's the time when life bursts forth;
Exciting, new beginnings:
Then summer, ripenings and warmth;
Beach holidays, and fun things!
When you start to feel a chill,
The days begin to shorten:
The greens turn gold, trees shed their leaves:
Behold the charms of autumn!
Not everyone enjoys the cold,
When winter winds blow icy:
Just draw the curtains, light your fires,
Cook stew pots, hot and spicy!

Corinne Lovell

AUTUMN

Autumn is a time of year,
when the leaves rustle in the breeze,
the best time of the year,
when the leaves change their colour to red,
bronze and gold,
oh how they look so very bold,
the rain falls heavily from the skies,
falling onto the leaves,
they must be crying,
because they are withering and dying.
Everyone will cheer,
when spring is here,
the leaves will gradually grow,
because we all love them so.

Joanna John

AUTUMN INTO MILLENNIUM

Changes in light,
The sun has earlier gone to sleep,
Receding,
Speeding on the canopy of night,
Impeding,
Hours of day to win dark's fight.

So light retreats,
Excited shadows leap from dimness,
Time for fun,
Another story born of grimness,
Night begun,
A frightened voice entreats.

Rose hips appear,
Shining like early Christmas lights,
Fruits of the rose,
Their last chance as this century goes,
To give delight,
Harvest of the fading year.

Yet will spring come,
Bring new mysteries along the way,
A birthday,
All may share in the millennium,
2000
Years, rings out across the land.

'Happy Returns',
New century like a parcel wrapped,
With great care,
So who will then unwrap the first layer,
In time trapped,
A gift, love, 'Happy Returns'.

Kathleen Mary Scatchard

WINTER

Murky days shorten and life starts to fade,
The chocolate tilled-earth, deeply overlaid,
Crimson swathed skies, on low sunlight glare,
Crows break the silence, rasping the air.

Dusk frowns down on rain-lashed streets,
Winds chime their tunes, ravaging beats,
Curtains closed tightly, comfortable glow,
High heels clatter loudly, on pavements below.

Flakes swirl and dance, a ballet for us all,
Low muffled noises, cushioning wall,
Empty dried husks, of finger and toe,
Land seems untouched, carpeted with snow.

The same old decay, from old year to new,
Annual thanksgiving or sorrow review,
Ongoing, nature recycles the rot,
Springtime promise, time never forgot.

Pat Derbyshire

Summer

Last year it rained! oh how we moaned!
What's happened to the sun? we groaned.
This year it's sunny! oh how we moan!
The garden needs the rain, we groan!

Whatever the weather God provides
It doesn't suit us all,
If every day was just the same
It would soon begin to pall.
And whatever would we talk about
When friends came round to call.

So enjoy the summer's light and sun
And wealth of coloured flowers,
And keep their memory in your mind
To brighten winter's hours.

Joan Gray

SPRING SENSES

I can see the birth of spring,
In primrose, bluebell and celadine.
In colours yellow, white and blue,
Which touch these eyes of mine.
I can hear the song of spring,
From skylark hovering high.
A cuckoo calling across the dunes,
Tells that March 21st has gone by.
I can smell the air of spring,
From new cut grass in lawnmower box.
On crocus saffron and in tulip heart,
Which greet the vernal equinox.
I can taste the joy of spring,
When winter's hold it first unlocks.

K P Watch

Autumn Dreams

The pile of fallen russet coloured leaves,
Danced their way down on the breeze.
Collecting conkers, the best always up high,
And the sycamore seeds, like helicopters fly.

As I watch the autumn come and go,
Still wondering at all it has to show.
And with all the changes that it starts,
It stirs dreams of change within my heart.

Sara Harris

LADIES OF THE SEASONS

Veiled in mist spring tiptoed in with her usual flair,
She drew sweet violets in her train and blossoms crowned her hair,
Her gown of lily crocus, narcissi, daffodil,
She walked upon a carpet green, over field and hill.

Silently, just as she came, so silently she went,
And summer sitting in her bower filled the air with scent,
Bedecked in roses, marguerites and every pretty flower,
She took the sun and morning dew and bathed in gentle shower.

But autumn, waiting round the bend with bustle and with lace,
Scattered petals, leaves and trees, once held in her embrace,
When she'd tired of playing with all her golden glow,
Winter laid her blanket down, of thistledown soft snow.

Her companion, the robin, hopped about with ease,
Showing off his red breast, knowing how to please,
As winter's brow still glistened bright a little snowdrop came,
And through the mist spring tiptoed in, sweet violets in her train.

Katie Hill

RAIN IN DECEMBER

Man in a bus shelter
smiling at the rain,
in a sleepy kind of way
on a day in December.

Cold in the bus shelter
where we sat without words,
as the birds huddled close
in a friendly kind of way.

No great ideas
in the cold bus shelter,
adverted and grey,
on a day in December.

As his cigarette burned
down to his fingers
he smiles at the rain
for no special reason.

Little icy puddles forming,
lorries go and to and fro,
splashing muddy water,
outside getting wet

And a man in a bus shelter
smiling at the rain
in a happy kind of way,
on a day in December.

Bridget Rayner

COMES NOVEMBER

The shades of autumn now appear
In russet, green and gold
The changing winds whip through the trees
That shiver with the cold.
The bluebirds find no hiding place
From fierce and driving rain
Those butterflies they all have gone
To whence begins life chain.
The morning frost escorts the dawn
And nights grow early dark
The loneliness of nature shows
O'er lea and field and park.
But some time soon the sun will shine
And promise hope anew
When spring on earth
Gives life its worth
Eternally on cue!

Harold Hyman

WINTER

Nights begin to shorten
Icicles appear
A chilly blast from northern winds
Says winter's drawing near

Fires are lit in abundance
As temperatures dip low
When dusk turns into darkness
Friends huddle round their glow

Autumn leaves, long fallen
Lie carpeting the ground
And birds have left for warmer climes
Where food stocks may be found

Jack Frost gets out his paintbrush
The world to cover white
He works away profusely
Making patterns in the night

Then the snow begins to fall
And children shout in glee
'Let's get the sledge out daddy
First ride belongs to me'

'We'll build a great big snowman
With hat made out of felt
And dress him in a long coat
Before he starts to melt'

I love the springtime newness
The summer and the fall
But nothing can compare to this
Winter has it all

P N Vout

My Place To Sit (Spring)

As I sit and observe
the bees and the birds
I relax and take it all in.

Thistles, old man's beard
the leaves are a blur,
they dance and whisper
as branches sway.

I notice the pigeons, the crows
and the tits, their tiny bodies
through the undergrowth flit.

The colours, the fresh smells,
the peace and hum of the bee,
an unspoilt paradise for me.

That's where I like to sit.

Paul Robards

Spring Again

Once more the threat of winter's snow
Diminishes in my mind
And tiny shoots and buds now show,
As trees and flowers of every kind
Wake up to spring's caress

The warmth that left me with the fall
Now slowly melts the frozen ground.
Faint to the ear I hear the call
Of ewes, to lambs that round them bound,
Full of life and zest

And as the dark of winter nights,
The bitter cold of frosted days,
Makes way to colour, warmth and light,
My wakened mind no longer plays
On thoughts that can depress

As fledgling birds wait in their nests
And blossom swells on countless trees,
My heart will ride upon the crest
Of springtime tides out on the sea,
And yearn for summer less.

Anne Goldson

SUMMER RAIN

Clouds massing together
In the evening twilight
A change in the weather
No doubt coming tonight;

Cirrostratus clouds begin to congest
Forming a ring round the moon,
Altocumulus moving in from the west
Indicating rain will come soon;

Caverns appear in the darkening cloudscape
Deep dark caves where troglodytes hide,
Mountainous contours, convoluted in shape,
Multicoloured spirals with pixies inside;

A series of air waves passing down stream
Descending in troughs and many a hollow,
Reflecting the last light of a setting sunbeam
As into the twilight the flight of a swallow;

The curtain of night is now falling fast,
The lamplights are shining down in the lane,
With 'castle wall' clouds the sky overcast
And on my face I can feel the first drop of rain.

Roy V Whitlock

Walking The Four Seasons

Walking hills in summer, quite dry the ground.
Between the trees, bright the shimmering sun.
Beneath the feet the now dead leaves give sounds
That stirs the thoughts, tho' trampled just for fun.

Autumn brings more pleasing walks, of times wet,
With air like wine to savour scenes anew.
Less time to laze as sun so early sets,
And squirrels scurry high on winter's cue.

Winter, sometimes grim, can atone with white,
Beware the ground for ankles are not strong.
The trees may crack with frozen sap so tight,
A blade of sun tells spring will not be long.

Walks in spring make fresh body, soul and mind
So venture new hills, they are there to find.

Edgar Wall

HIS PRESENCE

Can't you feel God's presence as each season comes and goes?
Can't you feel His love, His warmth, in the dark December snows?
Can't you feel His joy, when the buds burst forth each spring?
Can't you feel His tenderness, each day, in everything.

Jenny Eleftheriades

BEAUTY

Woven in this tapestry
Of brown and gold and green
A picture painted by the eye
Each day a different scene.

With a subtle touch of magic
Each shape is made to blend
Creating for each one who sees
A picture without end.

With gentle strokes of genius
Soft as a angel's kiss
Summer in all her glory
Has not beauty such as this.

Seen from every angle
In every kind of light
No where else in heaven or earth
Is there such a wondrous sight.

To stand before this vision
Its majesty you will find
Will hold you captive by its charm
And paint it in your mind.

It changes by the minute
Each year it's born anew
A gift given to so many
Accepted by so few.

Alone for us mere mortals
This beauty's set apart
Nature's yearly miracle
Autumn's work of art.

Christine Ormrod

YEAR

January came and went, it passed before my eyes,
When February did the same I stopped to realise.
I welcomed March with open arms and optimistic mind,
Then April followed very fast and disappeared behind.
May arrived, I watched it stop and linger by the way,
June appeared and carried on for ever and a day.
As July waited peacefully for August to appear,
September reared impatiently and made the passage clear.
October sallied onward, unhindered now and then,
November gathered speed until December came again.
As the year eroded, and time again was gone,
I wondered why I couldn't see the things that I had done.

Ian Coxall

WINTER'S AMBASSADOR

Imperceptibly, the aroma of air
Slips from sweet to sour,
As nature, gorged on summer's over-rich abundance,
Eructates its rank and bilious breath across the land.

Damp shrouded mornings infiltrate the mind,
Like clammy-fingered demons, to poke and prod,
Whisper slyly, then deposit,
Bleak thoughts of brooding and melancholy times.

Rain's richness, transmuted by osmotic journey
To poison, banishes to earth redundant leaves,
Where swept and ignominiously burned, they now
Pollute the very air they once refreshed.

So autumn, ambassador of soulless, withered winter,
Herald of dank and sullen days,
Harbinger of icy fingered mornings,
Once more pronounces black-capped judgement on the soul.

Barry Jones

AUTUMN

Death can be beautiful
just look at the trees!
Orange and scarlet and gold.
Colours hidden by summer's green
blaze forth against the autumn sky
with a shout of glory.
Fruiting over, harvest gathered in,
a space to play, to show their true colours
a wind blown dream time.
Watching one early morning
(my own mortality uppermost in my mind)
leaves, kissed by the rising sun
dropping in showers like topaz tears
covering the frosted earth with golden gauze
a brightly coloured carpet woven by the season.
Later, bare limbs will creak in bitter snows
learning endurance, testing time,
colour gone and dead to casual eyes.
But I have faith and will not mourn
for they merely sleep, so when spring comes
with warmer winds and busy worker bees,
branches will bud and flower once more repeating
season after season the familiar pattern
of archaic generations; store of genes.
But now, death can be beautiful;
just look at the trees!

Audrey Willis

SOUNDS OF SUMMER

Silver birch tentacles sway in summer breezes
As self conscious birds drop to feed on breadcrumbs
Sun toasted lying on the flaxen thirsting grasses

A scattering of surfacing ants
    frenetically rush in many directions
Confusing all spectators and
    avoiding silent predators

A sleeping feline lazily stretches
    causing a turbulence of flutterings
Panicking the dreaming fish shading
    under florescent pink and yellow lilies

The second hand clicks over the hour
Releasing a burst of inarticulate sounds
A swelling of voices, screaming and shouting
Immediately terrorising the senses
Oblivious the spring flowers of life pass
Leaving a trail of loitering littering

Warmth invades,
    sleep intrudes,
        peace pervades.

. . . a tremor, twitter, twitch, tickle,
    ears are paining, wings are fluttering,
    fur is raising and fins are darting,
    a sinister silver snout skims the sky
    as sound waves sear the atmosphere
    out of tune with those who dwell here.

Joy Adams

WAITING

Sunny day - misty mountain
Naked trees unclothed as yet -
How I'm waiting for the moment
When the spring has come at last
And winter's scourge has finally passed.

The dark brown earth I love to touch
And sift it through my fingers,
And see those buds above the soil -
They make worthwhile my hours of toil,
A touch of cold still lingers.

I close my eyes and list awhile
And a singing bird invades my brain,
His music lifts my heart above the clouds
And veils my dream in rainbow shrouds,
I know the flowers will bloom again.

Mary Josephine Devlin

SONG OF THE SEASONS

Remember the sun, the heat of the day
Children laugh as they go out to play
How we sipped our drinks, so sweet and cool,
And splashed about in the swimming pool.

When winter came with wind, rain and snow,
We wrapped ourselves up, faces aglow,
The trees shed their leaves, the birds searched for food,
We hurried straight home in Christmassy mood.

Spring comes at last with promise of sun,
The flowers nod their heads, having such fun,
The birds fly about with beaks full of food,
Everyone now is in jolly good mood.

Eileen Naish

AUTUMN LEAVES

Oh, that I would fall
So gracefully in death as
Autumn leaves. Duty

done. No requiem.
No fuss. No crimson pool or
anguished cry. No tear

or painless final
breath. But why your tree undress
with winter near? Her

toes to keep like toast,
maybe. But of your final
resting place, who knows?

Undignified, crushed
underfoot? Resurrected,
but fleetingly; to

pirouette bestride
the wind? Or if the swishing
bristle comes, perchance

could billow skyward.
But, if sun-kissed dry; oh, that
you might die as noble

Viking would.

James West

Winter's Day

Aw Maw, let me coorie intae the fire,
Ma feet's like lumps o' ice,
It's awfae dark this mornin',
An' Ah dinae think that's nice.

Aw Maw, will ye look oot the windae?
Dae ye see yon flakes o' snaw?
They're a' swirlin' an' dancin' an' birlin',
An' the gairden's a' white an' a'.

Aw Maw, whaur hiv ye pit ma jaickit?
Ah'm gaun oot tae play,
An' me an' Billy an' Jock an' Tam,
We'll hae braw fun the day.

Aw Maw, dae Ah hiv tae come in fur ma tea?
Ah'm haein' sic great muckle fun.
Jist look at the snawman we've built oan the gress,
An' we've made a smashing sledge run.

Aw Maw, dae Ah hiv tae gang ben tae ma bed?
Ah'm no' near ready tae sleep.
Can Ah gae oot tae play the morn again?
Ah'll jist gie ma snawman a peep.

Kate Machean

SUMMER HAAR

Softly and with delicate stealth it forms.
Coming after sunshine - a day's length or a week.
Hiding all things familiar under its protective cloak.
And what was sunlit is now so bleak.

Sallow, the colour of its Sunday best,
Gives no inspiration to those of artistic bent.
Would make small impact on canvas or silk,
And where is the joy in the foghorn's lament?

Mystery is its offering to the amateur sleuth
Whose paperback villains lurk in the chilly gloom,
Plotting misdeeds under cover of dew
While honest folk nestle in its temporary womb.

Helen Logie

SPRING AWAKENING

Chaffinches chattering, cheeky sparrows scattering;
Blackbirds hob-nobbing; magpies a-mobbing;
Apple trees blossoming begun.

Daffodils a-dancing; partridges prancing;
Starlings strutting; swifts on wires mustering;
And robins on the run.

Soft breezes sighing; flying geese a-crying;
Redwings resting; nightingales a-nesting;
Wagtails waddling in the mud.

Newborn lambs stumbling; honeybees bumbling;
Collared doves cooing; owls tu-whit tu-whooing;
Swallows swooping in the sun.

Woodpeckers whirling; skylarks a-swirling;
Petals unfurling; hedgehogs uncurling;
Blue tits rearing their young.

House martins building; frog spawn ponds a-gliding;
Thrushes sweetly singing; insects on air winging;
And winter is all done.

Spring has come.

Heida

It's A Mystery

It's a mystery this old world of ours
As we watch it unfold its powers
It's a mystery how the seasons flow
And how the tiny seeds and flowers grow
The wonder of seeing spring again
How nature ripens fields of grain

It's a mystery how we fall in love
Receiving blessings from above
How children come from nature's power
We watch them growing hour by hour
What creates them in our mould
To live their lives from young to old

What spreads the raindrops o'er the land
Is it nature's powerful hand?
The sun, the stars, the Milky Way
And how we remember yesterday
Who gives us eyes that we may see
The wonders of this mystery?

Who gives us faith that we may hope
As through dark day we have to grope?
To find our way into the light
Who gives us courage for the fight?
What makes us well when we are ill
And fills our heart with sweet goodwill?

We only know one thing for sure
The mystery deepens even more
As we try to understand
The wonders of God's mighty hand

J W Hewing

A Touch Of Frost

A touch of frost upon the ground,
The cool night air descends around,
Those warm hot summer days are past,
With the evening light now failing fast.

Birds' nests built high up in the trees,
Whose structural moulds keep out of the breeze,
That blows so freely in the evening light,
With shadows flickering from left to right.

The leaves have changed from green to gold,
Oak trees tall, shed their conker load,
These fall down upon the ground,
As excited children gather round.

All is safely gathered in,
Harvests passed, the grounds now thin,
With fresh new crops to come next year,
The farming community is in good cheer.

Trick or treat will soon be here,
Pumpkins, witches in traditional gear,
That's what makes our autumns bright,
With so much change in colour, a delight.

M J Swain

AUTUMN

As summertime slips gently by,
Days grow shorter and time seems to fly.
Crops to gather, preserves to make,
Summer's bounty there to take.

Blackberries waiting for you to pick,
Conkers to knock down with walking stick.
Rose hips, crab apples, acorns too,
Just to name but a few.

Isn't it marvellous how they all grow?
From tiny seeds set long ago.
Mushrooms now in field are found,
For you to gather as you walk around.

Squirrels gathering nuts to store,
Running back and forth with more.
Leaves now turning red and gold,
And the nights are getting cold.

Kids out celebrating Hallowe'en,
Witches and demons may be seen.
Time to curl up by the fire,
Till bedtime calls and you retire.

G W Bailey

OF WHAT WAS

The garden mocked in silence

> Everything hung
> Not in shame
> In raggedness

The last dead leaves
Broken snapped twigs
The empty bottle - flung aloft
Flower heads, with just a hint of glory past

All waiting for that helping hand

> To care
> To revitalise

The garden mocked in silence.

Doris Hoole

NOVEMBER RAIN

Grizzled rain, but beautiful,
Out of dull November sky,
Richly falling on the land
That drowsily prepares for rest.

Last broad leaves are now washed clean;
Jewel-like drops adhere at twigs'
Tips in wise variety
Of lulls between rich spectacles.

Grateful evergreens drink deep;
Battered summer lawns revive;
Blackbirds bathing in the pools
In satisfaction shake their wings.

Though with colours less intense,
Breezy nature still can smile
Gold and russet in the mist
Of our good year's late middle-age.

When one's happy, one can see
Beauty in the greyest things.
Rain descends to dampen earth,
But not our spirits or our sight.

Welcome, fresh and calming rain!
Cleanse our vistas of all dross,
Life-renewing source of strength,
As we meet winter's challenge now.

Anne Sanderson

DAYS

Days of daisies, poppies tall,
grasses in a meadow.

Days of blue skies, blue butterflies,
playing with your brothers.

Days of love with mother and father.
Days of cousins, aunts and uncles,
sitting on the beach.

Days of dancing, weddings, travelling to Malta
with your lover.

Days of love letters,
days of fun at your nana and grandad's house
with Diane and Maxine,
and your brothers.

Days of happiness with your husband
sitting in a boat on the river.

Days of bird song, let it go on forever.

Valerie Ryan

A Change In The Weather

The man arrived on time to inspect the house.
He stepped in,
And asked me how things were.
I had been prepared to be angry,
About jobs undone, or left unfinished,
But when he spoke, I could not go on
With assertiveness and demands,
Because he said that my husband had told him,
And I did not correct what he had said,
But let it settle around our walls,
Like a flurry of snow in summer,
And he left, not realising his mistake,
And I shut the door, as his feet dragged in the new weather outside.

Helen Allison

A Song For Summer

Can you see the flowers grow?
Can you mount a bird's wing?
Can you count the drops flowing in a stream?
God's love is so vast and so strong,
He who holds the stars in place.
And created everyone.

God's love, His love can hold me fast,
His arms can carry me through each day,
Now, I believe,
Trust in Him for your every need.
Surely, you really can!

Jenny Pearce

IMAGES OF AUTUMN

A pale sun materialises through
the gossamer veil of swirling mist
gaining momentum as the day progresses,
igniting hedgerow berries like
sparks of vermilion fire,
painting trees in myriad hues
forming tawny-dappled images
on the mirrored lake.
Tongues of fiery flame lick over
bracken-covered hillsides
turning brown to gold
enveloping the landscape in
a cloak of warmth.
Tangy wood-smoke hangs
in the still air,
drifting, nostril-tingling.
As evening approaches and day is ending
logs crackle and glowing embers
die in cottage hearths.
Cool air creeps in and the sun
sinks down over the horizon
like a vast conflagration.

John Taylor

HAIL, GLORIOUS DAY!
(Written in celebration of the start of a beautiful day)

Hail, glorious day - in bright array!
The dawn sun streaking in the morn sky
Heralds a new birth
Of expected joys.

The early birds arise and fly,
And morning mists do burn away
As quiet dark becomes activity -
Activity in light.

Night creatures hide,
And those which walk in day
Assume their world
Like kings ascending to a throne.

The flowers awake,
And with expectant faces
Presume the arrival of their winged visitors.

All greet this blessed orb -
The fount of life and light.

Thou has arrived!
Hail, glorious day!

Frank L Appleyard

SPRINGTIME IN ENGLAND

Oh joyous day which has just begun
Feel the warmth of the early sun.
Breathe in deeply the crisp sharp air
and happily dwell on this land so fair.
Take a gentle stroll down leafy lanes
and capture the magic of youth once again.
Climb a stile and look at the view
a breathtaking sight of azure blue.
Carpets of bluebells shimmering with dew
welcoming the hiker to pass on through.

Mollie Fribbens

Autumn Garden

The warm glass of gentle evening air,
A distillation of midday sun,
Spills out across my lazy lawn
And shakes the long stemmed roses,
Waiting to fill the vase with falling bloom.

Fussing small birds
Blue, green, yellow, brown -
Cling to dying and dead with ferocious zeal,
Picking quarrelsome food
From seeded stems.

Dizzy bees, bumbling insects
And gaudy butterflies
Launch carefully from fallen fruit,
As drunken as blackbirds
Amid crab-apple dew.

And the secret surface of speckled pool
Catches fire, as golden forms
Move indolent beneath, remembering -
Remembering the endlessness of ice to come
And sinking to deeper bed to wait for spring.

John F Petrie

The Last Rose

Evermore feeble fingerings
Of sunlight touch the land,
Yet fiercely defiant of the first frostings
Summer is still lingering.

Maybe the leaves have the kindest
Elemental guardians, allowing a
Glorious demise,
A shroud for each in bronze and gold.

The whispers of approaching winter
Reach the swallows and send them into farewell flight.
But some are slow to hear the news,
For some place, somewhere blooms the last rose.
Stem shivering slightly and leaves lost now
The bravest bud makes open invitation
To the misty air.

This rose, paled by the cooled light
To softly tinted icing sugar shades,
Stands in honoured, isolated splendour
The last and chosen one of this millennium.

Denise E Wain

The Harvest Tree

The tree so majestic dominates the scene,
Over the field where the corn has been.
The branches reaching up, tall and erect,
The leaves hiding blemishes, a secret well kept.
Its form casts a shadow on the now fallow field,
The earth is spent, having given its yield.
Recently the corn, so golden and neat
Was standing proudly for the farmer to reap.

Once felled by men with scythes and hooks,
The then bundled stems rose again as stooks.
Stood to dry by the children and women,
Who gleaned for grain to help with their living.
The crisp dry sheaves, by horse and wagon,
Were taken to the rick yard in readiness for threshing.

But now . . . into the field move machines and men
To bring this harvest to a timely end.
The burley combine harvester with its lumbering roar,
Stores the grain and spews out the straw.
This is baled, large stacks appear,
Then, as if by magic, all is cleared.
The field has supported life for centuries,
The tree, still proud, has its memories.

John A Gordon

The Year

Winter's night was long, the moon shone above,
Pavements sparkled frost was bitter, and love
Impervious to the freezing weather,
Thought evening would last forever.

Spring arrived and mist and rain
Damped branches which were again
Decked with blossom along the winding lane
They sheltered beneath a lofty plane.

Summer came and once more the sun
Kissed blue skies and life was full of fun
Discarding coats on scorching grass
They sat together, could this moment last?

September brings the dawn of winter
Evening fades to leave the after glow,
Home is warm and lasts forever;
They no longer trudge through winter snow.

Graham L

SEASONS

Where have all the swallows gone?
The gaudy bright butterflies that flittered at play.
Dragonflies with gossamer wings,
With the meadow lark, have flown away.

For Autumn has stretched out its greedy hand,
Plucking the last from Summer's veil.
A hush will soon fall over the land,
Heralding the start of a Winter's tale.

But Spring e'er long will awake anew,
Paving the way for Summer's gold.
The May fly will soar and the swallows return,
And nature's scenery will again unfold.

Doris E Farran

First Day Of Autumn

The first day of autumn has autumned
The sunshine and unacceptable humidity are gone
Hazy mist makes the trees look like mountains
Shrouded in mystery like some Middle Earth land
Drizzle so light you can hardly feel it
Touching your face but so gently you wonder if it was real
Like the blurred edges of a memory you always thought was a dream
I can see my breath's vapour, like a dragon I smoke the air
Mystery comes with the light, flitting mists
Covering the trees to make them look like Amazonian rainforest
Blurring their edges, obscuring their form, letting imagination free
Like alcohol vision it plays havoc with a familiar scene

Frankie Bell

SNOWING BLOWING, RAINING HARD

It is snowing, blowing, raining hard
Oh where is the sun on my birthday card
Though it is winter now for all to see
How many people will come to my birthday tea.

It is snowing, blowing, raining hard
Is it safe to walk or do we use the car?
What if we get lost or cannot find our way
Do we stay the night if we can find our way.

It is snowing, blowing, raining hard
Must we enjoy the evening using candlelight
In a place this big an old one can soon catch fright
Though it is full of laughter.

Keith L Powell

THE AUTUMN BLACKBERRY

The blackberry bush,
Natural, wild and beautiful,
A plant entangling and intertwining,
Growing and abundant,
Berries deep blue, massed
Between dark green leaves
And prickles protecting
Its harvest glory.
Now golden and brown,
Fruit picked and eaten
The blackberry bush
Shines in majestic colour,
Bathed in the deep orange
Sunset of autumn.

Joan E Blissett

AUTUMN GLORY

Red and gold and amber
Leaves fall upon the ground.
Squirrels run and clamber
Their winter store is found.
The nights grow chill, the moon is bright
An owl hoots in the trees.
Summer birds are leaving us
For warmer climes than these.
The golden sun still warms the earth
When morning mists have past,
Shining on the little pearls
That nestle in the grass.
There's heather on the hillside
Blue, amethyst and white,
Mother Nature's woven her spell
A carpet of delight
This is Autumn glory
With sunshine and with rain
And with her quiet wisdom
Still lovely once again.

Mary Rose Samm

MIRACLE

Such a wondrous thing is spring,
You almost hear the bluebells ring,
The furtive movement of something.
A butterfly with painted wing,
Blackbird calling, born to sing.

A fawn in secret woodland prancing,
A stream that tripping laughing dancing
Wends its way through worlds entrancing,
Through dappled woods and fields advancing,
A gentle magic world enhancing.

Forget-me-nots and daisies bearing
Crowns of beauty, almost daring,
Children playing, laughing, tearing
Through the brambles never fearing,
Tumbling, falling, never hearing,
A cuckoo's call so soft endearing.

Beneath the ground a tiny quaking,
Deep dark burrows then forsaking,
Little animals are shaking
Winter's sleep away and taking,
Time to watch the world awakening,
To the glory of a springtime's making.

Tony Coyle

AUTUMN

Autumn days crisp and clear
Are what I look forward to
This is the only time of year
When I could never feel blue.

Autumn mists gently falling
Bringing in the morning dew
Spiders' webs strung like pearls
Trees in gowns of various hue.

Autumn leaves of different colours
Brightening up our humdrum days
Green and brown, red and gold
Glistening with the sunshine's rays.

Autumn days I like the best
Pleasant memories I recall
Sometimes chilly, sometimes warm
In autumn - season of the fall.

And so the season slowly passes
Nature starts to slow things down
But the autumn season is for me
The real jewel in the crown.

D Linnett

THANKSGIVING

The lengthening nights and shortening days,
Foretell the winter's drawing nigh,
And leaves in drifts of colour lay
Where autumn winds do sough and sigh.

Beneath the hedgerows, now adorned,
In berries black and deep blood-red,
Entwined in bramble, briar and thorn,
The hedgehog builds its winter bed.

A first frost, silvered, on the grass,
And overhead a wide blue sky,
Air crystal clear, small clouds float past,
And echoing the pheasants' cry.

While beech nuts fall and conkers swell,
And toadstools thrust through mossy banks,
And rabbits scamper in the dell,
The harvest gatherers give thanks.

In churches decked with festive fare,
Sheaves and wreaths with leaves entwined,
And flowers and fruit in mountains high,
We leave the summer far behind.

Jim Sargant

AUTUMNAL THOUGHTS

Thoughts of autumn burning in my mind.
Fiery red, gold and brown of deciduous
leaves colouring my imagination, igniting
it with wonder.

Dreams of inhabiting an autumn
forest. Bathing in all that scarlet and
yellow glory. Touching branches,
entering tree trunks.

Basking in soft warmth from a late autumn
sun. Weak but beautiful light wrapping
everything in shimmering blanket of
varying colours.

Sun strengthening unexpectedly, his
sparkling jewelled cloak hurled over trees
and branches. Green plants becoming gems also
as they flash like emeralds amongst shining
leaves akin to rubies and amethysts.

Now sun's presence glows even brighter,
though only momentarily, as he casts his
golden crown towards Earth in homage
to autumn's beauty.

Terry Burrows

THE LAUGHABLES

You have your sunshine rain
I'll have my rain.
Dress that dress
Smile that smile
Smell those smells.
I truly hate you.
I stare to oblivion
Raising a storm in my heart
But my tranquil eyes will hide it.
Confinement is solitude
A saver of torment,
Misjudged.
I'm crossing now to Rainbow Land
And teardrops are the rain
Where sunflowers touch the sky . . .

Louise O'Keeffe

REMEMBER WINTER

Remember the slippery playground
On a frosty winter morning,
When your breath came out in short white puffs
As you called and shouted to each other,
And tried to keep your balance
While muffled in coats, scarves and gloves.

Remember the colourful cocoon of the classroom
Where drowsy warmth blotted out the winter day.
Where you looked, wide-eyed, as the first flakes of snow
Fell lazily past the window,
Floating twisting and turning, to settle
Like frosted icing on the frozen ground.

Remember going-home time,
When you were met by mums with icy fingers
And little brothers and sister
With noses red and shiny from the cold;
And how you went with bags on backs
Slipping and sliding down the path.

Remember looking back at the school
In the winter dusk, its yellow lights
Illuminating the falling snow,
And how you knew that it was just sitting and waiting,
Waiting for you to come again tomorrow,
To share in its magic.

Patricia Harding

THE BEST THINGS IN LIFE ARE FREE

The best things in life are definitely free
And many have found this so to be:
The cheery sound of a dawn chorus filling the air
With beautiful song from everywhere;
The comfort of the sun rising majestic and round
Giving light and warmth to all around;
The pretty morning dewdrops sparkling in the sun -
Diamonds to treasure for everyone;
The daytime freshness of a gentle rain -
Cleansing and quenching the earth once again;
The glory of a garden with flowers and trees
Moving and dancing in a warm summer breeze;
The joy of a smile from someone dear,
Knowing their heart to yours is near;
The pleasure of walking along a seashore with a friend -
Not wanting the footprints to come to an end;
The delight of the countryside - fresh and green,
Offering beauty and rest that's so serene;
The splendour of the hills - secure and strong -
A promise of God's love as we journey along;
The grandeur of a waterfall cascading below -
A picture of God's love that will always overflow;
The magnificence of a sunset - orange, red and gold -
A reminder of the life to come, where we'll not grow old;
The wonder of the heavens under a clear night sky,
Where Jesus Christ descended from, so He for all could die;
Just two millennia now ago, this loving act took place
And the very best thing of all in life, is God's amazing grace!

Brenda Irene Piper

SUBMISSIONS INVITED
SOMETHING FOR EVERYONE

POETRY NOW 2000 - Any subject, any style, any time.

WOMENSWORDS 2000 - Strictly women, have your say the female way!

STRONGWORDS 2000 - Warning! Age restriction, must be between 16-24, opinionated and have strong views. (Not for the faint-hearted)

All poems no longer than 30 lines.
Always welcome! No fee!
Cash Prizes to be won!

Mark your envelope (eg *Poetry Now*) **2000**
Send to:
Forward Press Ltd
Remus House, Coltsfoot Drive,
Woodston,
Peterborough, PE2 9JX

OVER £10,000 POETRY PRIZES TO BE WON!

Judging will take place in October 2000